And I Did...

SUSAN D. CRUM

And I Did...
Susan D. Crum

Published August 2014
Second printing April 2023
Express Editions
Imprint of Jan-Carol Publishing, Inc
All rights reserved
Copyright © Jan-Carol Publishing, Inc.
Book Design: Tara Sizemore

This book may not be reproduced in whole or part,
in any matter whatsoever without written permission,
with the exception of brief quotations within book reviews or articles.

ISBN: 978-1-939289-47-6
Library of Congress Control Number: 2014948626

You may contact the publisher:
Jan-Carol Publishing, Inc
PO Box 701
Johnson City, TN 37605
E-mail: publisher@jancarolpublishing.com
Website: jancarolpublishing.com

I dedicate my book And I Did...
in memory of my mother, Mary Katherine Crum,
whose courage has inspired me to overcome adversities in my life.
I will forever remember her touch when I was hurt,
the way she held me when I cried,
her boundless unconditional love for me, her dry sense of humor,
and her lovely smile and infectious laugh.
Most of all, I remember her love for God,
which she demonstrated in her own unobtrusive, unassuming way.

She touched many young lives while working in the Greeneville (TN) City School System, but the life she touched the most was mine. I was always honored Mrs. Crum was "Mom" to me.

My mother was highly revered in my eyes if for only one reason... she married the kind of man I always wanted to marry. I'm glad she encouraged me to practice patience, as I never thought I could ever meet a man like my father. And I did!

I wonder if she thought I'd fulfill my dream of being a motivational speaker? Yeah, probably. She often told me I set the bar too high for myself. And maybe I did. But I realized she didn't want to see me fail. So as not to disappoint her or myself, I conjured up the strength to reach it. And I did!

My mom's love and memory live on in my heart, as I will forever be grateful for her believing in me to continue writing. I am so blessed she was able to attend the launch party of my first book, *Only to Susan*, on my birthday (April 1) in 2012. Many of you know one of my favorite mottos is *Dream–Dream Big*, so Mom's birthday card to me that day was absolutely perfect. It read:

Happy Birthday to a Wonderful You!

- D – Dare all your dreams
- A – Always believe in yourself
- U – Uncover hidden talents
- G – Go on adventures
- H – Have fun and be happy
- T – Treasure tiny miracles
- E – Embrace Life
- R – Reach for the stars

May all your dreams come true, on your birthday and always.
Love you! Mom

LETTER TO THE READER

When I published *Only to Susan* in 2012, I marked *write book* off my bucket list. However, that whole process took on a much deeper meaning for me. I realized I wanted to inspire and encourage others to achieve their dreams, and not just to dream, but to dream big!

Since that time, my life has been an incredible experience, filled with both trials and triumphs. Through *And I Did...*, I want everyone who endures adversities—no matter how big or small—to know you too can be an overcomer. Don't miss out on life because you give up or give in too soon during the anguish in the midst of the battle. Even when we want to quit, know God can carry you through and can do what we can't do for ourselves. I love the message in Romans 8:28: *And we know that in all things God works for the good of those who love him, who have been called according to his purpose.*

Another item on my bucket list was to be a motivational speaker. Praises to God, this dream also is finally coming true—but again, not without the cost of several traumatic life experiences. However, I have learned to not ask God *why* such things happen but instead to ask *how* can I use them to glorify Him? I am asking Him to equip me to be a beacon of light and hope to others.

Now when I'm faced with fear, I can summon up the courage to fight—and fight to win. Now looking back over my life, I can say, "And I did!" And you can too!

Best regards,
Susan

ACKNOWLEDGMENTS

I would like to express my appreciation

To Janie C. Jessee, publisher/CEO, Jan-Carol Publishing, Inc, for the opportunity she gave me by first considering my manuscript and then accepting it, becoming my first publisher. I also wish to thank Jan-Carol staff members for their contributions to my inspiration and for their knowledge and other help in making this book a reality.

To Austin, my hero. You are an incredible young man and father, who I am very proud of and love more than life itself. Thank you for supporting me as I share our story, our challenges, which may resonate with women from all walks of life.

To Pete, my true North Star...the love of my life. What a Godsend you are...your unrelenting support of me and my dreams enables us to watch them come true—together. Thank you for the chapters of our lives we have already written and for the many chapters that await us.

And finally, I am grateful to God for the adversities in my life, a place where He has shown himself to be so kind, strong, and faithful. It has been through these difficult times my trust in Him and my faith have become as strong as they've ever been. As a result, I know I can find my way through the darkest of nights. I remain joyfully expectant of God's big plans in my life.

FOREWORD

Once upon a time—uuuuuhm, no. How many times did we hear or read those words as children?

It was a beautiful, summer's day—no. Don't like that one either. Besides, that makes me think of being on the beach while writing my book, not in the mountains of East Tennessee... speaking of....

It was a beautiful summer's day in the mountains—no, just doesn't have the same ring, does it?

Before the sparkly glitter fairies—surprisingly, that's not it. As you may know, I love wearing my glitter, but fairies????

In the year of 2014—no, no, no! Certainly not that one.

Obviously it can be difficult, at best, to start a beginning—the beginning of a chapter in a book or even the beginning of a chapter in life. At the first of this year, I challenged many of you to choose a word, a word you would aspire to describe your life when reflecting over the year of 2014. Mine? New-beginnings. OK, I cheated a bit. It is two words, thus the hyphen—but that is my word. New-beginnings is the word I'm going to use to describe my life while looking back over 2014 on New Year's Eve.

What is your one word? Now, I'm not talking about your New Year's resolutions and bucket lists. Those are excellent ways in which to strive to create change in your life and provide you with dreams, big dreams to reach for. I have those, too! But I'm talking about one word...OK, maybe two with a hyphen. If you know what that word is, WRITE IT DOWN–right now before you read another word. And try to write it on an index card–a colored index card, if you have one handy. Index cards are a bit sturdier than just paper. Why write it down? We are more likely to remember it and look at it more frequently. Then be sure and put your index card in your Bible, on your computer screen, in your wallet...somewhere where you will see it often. Then finally, share that word with someone you trust, such as your spouse, best friend, etc. We frequently share our progress regarding our one word during "Saturdays with Susan." OK, enough about your one word–back to the beginnings of the chapters in our lives.

Have you ever had a hard time getting a "chapter" started in life? You know–you just needed a start, maybe a break, in life? Then the rest of the words and chapters could possibly begin to just fall into place. Do you jog? If you do, would you agree the hardest part is getting started? A friend recently shared with me he, too, wants to write a book. I told him he'd never finish it if he didn't start it. Often the hardest part, right? I saw him about a week later and guess what? He had started his book! So I then encouraged him to keep writing! You know, once those first steps are achieved, we should sit back, with a sense of accomplishment and tell ourselves, "I always wanted to begin _____ (you fill in the blank)." Remember, you have to decide to begin the first chapter in achieving that dream. And when you do, pretty soon you will look back over time and say, "And I did!" You overcame all the obstacles, all the naysayers, to achieve your dreams. You, my friend, are/can be an overcomer.

Speaking of overcomers, following are a few short stories friends have shared with me about being an overcomer that I too want to share with you in hopes you will find inspiration. Remember, it is not how you start, it's how you finish. And they too can look back with much pride and say, "And I did."

I grew up feeling that whatever I did was not good enough, feeling like a failure in all I did. Neither of my parents graduated high school; my brothers were in constant trouble with the law and never graduated. I never graduated high school, but I now have two associate degrees and a BA. All three degrees were received with high honors. My mother died before I earned my first degree, and my father died while I was working on my second. I started my adult life as a single welfare mom—in the eyes of many that is all I would ever be. I overcame generations of poverty to live the legacy of "you can do it at any age." I got my BA in my 40s. That is my story. (Beverly Mahler, Greeneville, TN)

Another story of inspiration:
Something I can look back on and say that "I did it"—I enjoy writing fiction. I had written a few novellas and handed a few to some friends to read. I never, ever had an inclination to be published. But one friend in particular urged me to do it, so I said, "What the hey?" My book, containing six novellas, has been published. People seem to enjoy it, and it has received a few very nice reviews on Amazon. This has provided me with a decent sense of accomplishment. (Stuart Schwartz, Guadalajara, Jalisco)

A few other stories of inspiration I want to share:
We moved to East Tennessee without knowing a soul and have made a great life for us here! (Beverly Selmeski, Greeneville, TN)

AND I DID...

Moved to Greeneville from New Orleans without knowing anyone and have met some great people! (Dorothy Burnamster, Greeneville, TN)

When I was young, I always wanted to be a veterinarian, but I instead made a career out of teaching. It was absolutely the right choice for me...to go to work and love what you do for 37 years was a blessing. (Patricia Brady, Greeneville, TN)

I graduated from college with honors at 35 while working a full-time job and raising a child. (Deb Davis, Greeneville, TN)

I am committed to losing the weight, committed to keeping it off, committed to getting some sort of exercise 3 or 4 times a week. To some, small potatoes. To me, a big old harvest of 'em. (Lisa Stabler, Athens, GA)

And check out these two (both from Joyce Hopson, Greeneville, TN):

I had already obtained my master's degree in education, but several years later, I felt that the Lord was directing me back to college and showing me His plans for my life as a mental health counselor. So, in my mid-40s, I followed His lead to obtain my second master's degree (this one in counseling), went on to complete an extensive internship (while being married and working full-time), and completed all exams for state licensure. Today I enjoy a rewarding career and ministry in helping others deal with difficulties in life. And I did!

About 25 years ago, a job I had was affecting my health severely. My pulmonologist suggested I get a treadmill to work on increasing my oxygen capacity. Being obese did not help my breathing problems or make it easy to walk on that treadmill. When I started walking on that treadmill, 5 minutes at a very slow speed, it made me feel as though I would literally die. I would gasp and wheeze for air. My lungs have come a long way! Thank God! Through time and various helps, my lung issues healed. Secretly, I had always admired runners and wished that I could be a runner. Last year, I began working on my weight issues. I have lost 80 pounds so far, and with excitement, I can say that I am a runner. I completed three 5K races in the fall last year, and I have my first 5K of 2014 in two weeks. And I did! Oh, and I have a goal of running a half marathon (13.1 miles) this fall!

All of these personal stories are stories of real people who are not ordinary. These are stories about extraordinary people, just like you, just like me, who had a desire to accomplish something despite difficult times—and they did it! They were determined to succeed and be overcomers in life. They had the courage to look fear in the face and do it anyway. They didn't give up. They didn't let others take away their dreams. And all of these individuals, like myself, can look back and proudly say, "And I did!"

For these individuals, their opening lines have begun the first of many chapters in their lives. People like this don't just overcome challenges in life. They become examples to others, impressing others to find the words to begin their own chapters—whether they need to lose weight, decide upon or change a career, go back to school, publish a book, or make a life-changing move for them and their families.

AND I DID...

And you know what? Sometimes you don't even realize you've actually written many chapters of your life before you can even reread the first chapter. Maybe it's taken the rest of the chapters to truly understand what the first chapter said, what it meant. And in some cases, maybe you now can fill in the blanks you left behind during those times you just didn't understand.

CHAPTER 1

Three years later, sitting in the same room, in the same seat, I found myself going through much of the same routine, asking myself many of the same questions for which I had no answers. Since January 2010, the answers to some of my questions have been revealed. Yet some remain, and I have decided some will always remain.

As I continue to grow in my relationship with God, I realize He really expects us to trust Him when we don't understand. These are not just words our parents, grandparents, or ministers have told us: God told us in His word. But like everyone else, I'm human, and there have been times in my life when it was incredibly hard to trust God, especially when I had no clarity of understanding. And here I find myself, three years later, with more questions being added to my exhausted mental list. Things I don't understand—I don't understand His timing, His plan. All of this is only complicating the various, twirling thoughts in my head. I really did not know what to do, but I found myself at a point in my life where I realized, having overcome other adversities in my life, maybe I truly was trusting God, trusting Him completely. And I did.

AND I DID...

I was tired, so tired it hurt—physically and mentally. Have you ever felt that way? So tired you couldn't even think? Unlike my father's unexpected and sudden passing, we knew this day was coming for my mother. Having lost both parents under very different circumstances, I can attest you are never ready, nor is it any easier when you know their time is nigh.

As an only child and single mom, losing my father at the age of 39 then my mother at 42, I felt orphaned. The emptiness inside of me was unexplainable. The safety net under me had been removed, but I had to continue walking the high wire of life. When I looked down, I felt scared. All of a sudden, I felt completely alone in this big ole world. But thankfully, I had my son, Austin, and more importantly, we had God in our lives.

CHAPTER 2

It was Friday, February 18, 2013. I received a phone call that morning from the nursing home, informing me Mom's condition had worsened significantly overnight. The nurse suggested we make arrangements to be with her, as they did not think she would last much longer. I called Charlotte, my mother's first cousin, who had been more like a sister to Mom, and shared the news with her. Charlotte had also been my support during the last few months since Mom's health condition had continued to decline. This call was not a surprise, as we all had stood by, helpless, watching Mom's strength continue to wane...daily. We spent much of Friday and Saturday by her side. At this point, my mother was nonresponsive, yet her eyes remained open, and they assured me she could hear us. Although we tried to talk to her and comfort her, there was no evidence she heard or even felt our presence.

As difficult as this was, I had a peace in my heart. I believe the peace came from the fact I had done what I thought was best for my mother's care as her health had dramatically declined during the last couple of months. Plus, several weeks ago, we had the most touching mother-daughter talk. We said what needed to be said, as well as what we wanted to say. We shed a lot of tears and even laughed a bit. Mom and I always enjoyed our laughter, whether it

AND I DID...

was in church trying to compose ourselves, or when we'd get lost on one of our mother-daughter shopping adventures, or when an ocean wave would take her under with nothing but her backside in view. During our 42 years, we shared a lot of laughs...many times accompanied with tears streaming down our cheeks, finding their way in and around our cheesy ear-to-ear grins. I loved my mom's smile.

Especially after having such a touching mother-daughter moment, I never felt I was being held back because of words left unsaid, nor do I believe my Mom held on to any feelings. And most importantly, I had peace knowing my mother was a child of God. Soon she would be reunited with my father in Heaven, where she would no longer be in pain.

The last three months had been incredibly difficult. In October, my mother had thankfully initiated a conversation I'd wanted to have with her for a long time. I had actually mentioned this subject shortly after my father passed, but Mom quickly assured me she was perfectly capable of taking care of herself. Wow! Isn't it difficult when the roles of parents and children begin to transform? Although I completely disagreed with her on several issues, I had the gratification should anything happen to her at home, I had had her best interests at heart, and thus I had a peace of heart. Even after this matter-of-fact conversation, I continued to hint around at times, trying to express my concern as I knew it wasn't safe for her to be alone. When I did hint around, she would quickly stop me, somewhat defensively, assuring me she was managing just fine. Ever had those moments? I bet you have.

But I have to give my mom a lot of credit. She actually did pretty well for about two years. My mother was a strong woman. And thank God for her friends and neighbors, who would take her to doctor's appointments and look after her. And I especially thank God for watching over Mom when she chose to drive herself to the doctor or grocery store or to the dump—yes, the dump—to haul off her trash. Where we lived, we had to take our own trash to the convenience center. She was so funny. While at work, I'd often get a phone call or voicemail from Mom, telling me she was leaving to take the trash, which was located about a mile away. And guess what? She'd call me again when she returned. But at least I knew she was home safely!

I was grateful for the day when she finally became resigned to the fact it was not a good idea to drive any longer. In addition, she came to realization on her own she should get a medical alert button to wear around her neck. Mom had had a couple of really bad falls, which resulted in trips to the ER and several stitches. With the severe neuropathy in her hands and feet she lived with daily, it was difficult for her to know if and where her feet were planted as she walked. I had suggested Mom get a medical alert shortly after my father passed, but she, like most of us, came to realization on her own terms. That finally gave me somewhat of a peace since I could not always be there with her.

But soon after Mom got the medical alert button, things began changing rapidly. It quickly became very difficult for her to get out of bed. I even started leaving bottled water in a cooler by her bed so she could at least have something to drink. I was trying to make everything as convenient and easy as possible. But then, Mom began electing not to eat and she knew she could no longer take care of herself. As a result, we discussed options for her healthcare, and I agreed with her recommendation, which was to pursue an assisted-living facility.

CHAPTER 3

I called one of two assisted-living facilities in our community. The first one I called had no availability. We were disappointed, as we knew the director there. Nonetheless, the second one I called would have availability in a few days. So, we agreed to pursue this option. Mom asked I call Charlotte, and once again, she came.

Later that afternoon, a representative from the assisted-living facility was there...in Mom's home, by her bedside...discussing the possibility of her residency at the facility. We were very impressed, and my mother made most of the decisions. For once, I sat back and listened. Although I knew without a doubt this was best for my mother, it broke my heart. Within a few hours, all of the arrangements had been made, and papers were signed for my mother to move in a few days. Mom had also told Charlotte and me she was no longer going to take chemo or radiation treatments. Her radiology oncologist had recently found more lesions in her back from her multiple myeloma, which we felt was causing most of her pain, but the treatments were apparently aggravating her sciatic nerve. Neither one of us pressed. If that was Mom's wish, we would support her and try to make her as comfortable and well-cared-for as possible.

Unfortunately, the very next morning when I went by before going to work to check on Mom, I heard her before I saw her—she was in excruciating pain. I called 911 and an ambulance arrived to transport her to the hospital. As they took Mom out of her house on the gurney, somehow I knew my mother would never return home to the house she and my father built in 1970...the house I grew up in. The house where I learned to walk, talk, watch Hee-Haw with a big bowl of popcorn on Saturday nights, work puzzles with my mom when it snowed, appreciate the smell of cornbread, practice my piano when I refused to wash dishes, and sing "You Light Up My Life" with my record player that played 45s. Remember those? If you do, then you're at least as old as I am! If not, ask your parents or grandparents. But a few of the most precious moments in this house are where, with my parents help, I learned to pray and read my Bible. The same house where I was not always allowed in the living room—yet when Austin came along, he had free rein. Really???

As I went back in the house to ensure I had everything, I stood in the den...it was so quiet. As I looked around, succumbing to a 360 degree view from where my feet were planted, there was an immediate feeling, a feeling of emptiness. Dad wasn't there to walk down the hall to say, "Hey, gal," and now my mom would not be there to make her infamous fudge at Christmas. It was as empty as I could ever imagine a place of emptiness could feel. My father was gone. Now my mother was leaving. I all but sprinted out the door, closing it behind me while making sure I had all of my mother's things, hoping I'd never have to open that door again.

After my mom was evaluated in the emergency room, we were told there was nothing more they could do. She was in so much pain. Yes, she had been seen in the ER and admitted several times within the last few months, but I told them I couldn't take her home in this condition. I had to do something until we could move her to the assisted living facility in a few days...I needed time.

AND I DID...

I contacted the hospital administrator and case manager, both of whom are friends of mine, desperately reaching out to them for guidance. It appeared our only way for mom to be admitted was under the care of hospice, and knowing this was my only option, I agreed. About the only thing left to do was to control her pain, and I was determined to do all I could to ensure that happened—and I did.

CHAPTER 4

Shortly after she was admitted into the hospital, Mom quickly became confused and began hallucinating. I had heard stories of this behavior, but never thought I'd have to experience it with a loved one. In an effort to control her pain, she was on quite a bit of pain medication, which we attributed partially to her behavior. However, I didn't want her to be in pain. What a difficult predicament to be in...especially when it's your mother.

Having no experience, I tried hard to convince my mother otherwise when she was telling me something I knew was not true. One evening our conversation became very emotional for me as my mother became upset with me when I was trying to explain a situation had not happened. While one of the nurses continued talking to Mom, the other nurse nonchalantly motioned for me to follow her out of the room—and I did. The nurse assured me what Mom thought was happening in her mind was, in fact, really happening. "And I'm just supposed to go with it?" I cried out to the nurse in despair. And her reply? "Yes." That was one of the most difficult times for me because for the first time, even though she was my mother, she was not my mother.

Many times during this stay in the hospital, I told myself Mom would never make it to the assisted living facility. Family

AND I DID...

and friends who came by to see her concurred with my thought. Given her continued health decline, both physically and mentally, I didn't know how much longer she could hold on. Mom repeatedly made it clear she was tired and she wanted to be with my father once again...that's all she wanted. As hard as it was for me, I too wanted that for her—no more pain, no more suffering, no more sorrow. My mother had battled multiple myeloma cancer since 2007. In addition to her other health problems, I always feared the cancer would not kill her but she would grieve herself to death. She even repeatedly asked me and others not to pray for her healing.

The staff at the assisted living facility was so kind and willing to work with us to hold her room during her hospitalization, but there were several times I questioned the move, given her condition. Could they adequately take care of her there? Did she need to be in a more skilled nursing facility? But once again, I wanted to honor her request to go to the assisted-living facility first—a decision she made with a sound, cognitive mind. If it didn't work out, I'd have the contentment of knowing we tried. But now, I knew my mother just wanted to go home...not to her earthly home on the Asheville Highway where I grew up, but to her heavenly home where she would be reunited with my father.

CHAPTER 5

About ten days later, Mom's condition had improved to where we felt she could be discharged from the hospital and transferred to the assisted-living facility. She was in a good state of mind on this particular evening. She even flirted with the paramedics who were transporting her! I was so embarrassed! As we arrived at the facility, she was even sitting up in the gurney, waving to the residents in the foyer as she was wheeled down the hallway to her room. It reminded me of a crowned princess waving to the crowds lined up on the street to watch the annual Christmas parade. She even had the wave pretty down pat! I thought to myself *this move could not have gone any better—thank you, God.*

Thanks to several of my friends we had her room furnished with a bed, dresser, nightstand, and her television from home, plus pictures of Austin upon her arrival. My mom loved to watch college basketball, especially University of Tennessee and University of Connecticut. Yes...that is correct—not a typo. I met Coach Auriemma, better known as Geno, at a game in Georgetown—but that's all another story. I always enjoyed teasing Mom she chose her favorite basketball teams by how handsome the coaches were. Nonetheless, I told Geno about his biggest fan in Tennessee. He told me he couldn't believe he had any fans in Tennessee! I assured

AND I DID...

him he had two—my Mom was one and my friend, Rebecca, who was with me, was the other. We had our pictures made together, and I think my mom treasured that picture of Geno and me as much as the picture of me the day I was born.

Unfortunately, things again changed—quickly. Mom had no desire to watch college basketball or anything. Her confusion and hallucination began to reoccur, and this time they were even worse. It was not uncommon for me to receive not one, but multiple, phone calls during the night. I even tried having a sitter with her at night. The fact someone, a stranger, was in the room with her, just sitting there, made the situation even more difficult. So that lasted all of one night. Mom wore a call button around her neck, but I don't think she ever understood how to push it, nor was she capable of pushing it if she needed something. A few times she would even hold it up to her ear, thinking it was her cell phone! Bless her heart....

You know, every day I would walk in and see residents interacting with one another by the fireplace. It broke my heart Mom could not participate and enjoy their company. Except for the several trips to the ER, she never left her room from the minute she arrived until the day we moved her out, as she could not even get out of bed without assistance. Although being the strong-minded and strong-willed mother she was, she often did get out of bed—only to find herself in the floor trying to scoot to her destination. And only God knew where she was headed. Most days, the staff usually got her to agree to sit in her recliner so she could sit up for at least a while. The staff would also encourage and even try to help her eat. Most of the time she refused. The only thing she wanted was water...ice water. And when I was there, I always made sure she had some.

After multiple trips to the emergency room, the ER doctor pulled me aside, advising me the best thing I could do was move my mother to a skilled-nursing facility. I tried to reason with the doctor, insisting she was typically transported to the ER when a staff member would find her in the floor. Not seeing her fall, it was their policy to transport the resident. Yet, I knew the ER doctor was right...plus my compromise was rather weak. I had wrestled with this same dilemma prior to moving her to the assisted living. The thought of my mother telling me to never put her in a nursing home was weighing heavy on my heart. I had knots on top of knots in my stomach. Even though the assisted-living facility was perfect in every way, from the caring staff to her room, everyone knew she needed to be at a skilled-nursing facility, including me.

The ER doctor did admit my mother, as she had a fever, and this gave me time to make preparations to have her moved to a nursing home. Charlotte and I visited a couple of the nursing homes before I decided on the one for Mom. When she was in her right mind making decisions about the assisted living facility, she was rather adamant she wanted a private room. So to honor her wish, I too wanted her to have a private room in a nursing home, as well.

During the throes of Mom being in the hospital and moving to the skilled nursing facility, my dear friends and I once again found ourselves about a month later moving all of her belongings back to my house from the assisted-living facility. Her room in the nursing home was mostly furnished.

Ironically, the nursing home we selected is the same one she'd, unfortunately, had to move her mother to many years ago. I hoped and prayed she would not recognize the facility, since she had instructed me to never put her in a nursing home. The anguish I was experiencing through all of this suddenly increased to an all-time high, yet I knew this was best for my mother, as neither I—nor anyone else—could take care of her at home as she had far surpassed that level of care.

One day, during this hospitalization (which would be her last), Mom and I had the most precious conversation. Her mind was clear, and we held hands and cried and talked and cried some more. She would occasionally ask me, "What will you and Austin do?" I always assured her we'd be fine. I felt like she was holding on to something, and we were that something. Even though I told her we'd be fine, I had no idea how we'd be fine, but what I did know is God would take care of us, as my faith and trust were in Him. Although this was a moment I will never forget, I feared the soon, forthcoming news of moving her to a skilled-nursing facility would not go over very well…at all.

The hospitalist had discussed sharing this news with my mother the day she was being discharged so I wouldn't take the brunt. When he told her, I don't think she understood completely, as she began to ask me questions…questions I did not want to answer—but I did. Of course, this day was not unlike most days. One minute her mind seemed clear…the next minute, not so much.

Later that afternoon, the paramedics came to transport her. She was not as flirtatious this time. She was more solemn—yet content. Charlotte and I followed the ambulance to the nursing home and then helped her get settled in her room. Once again, it could not have gone any better, but I knew harder days were yet to come. I just didn't expect them to start the next morning. But the level of care she received there was incredible. I have always thought it takes a special person to work in health care. It takes an even more special person to work with patients like my mother. They spoiled her to death…literally, until her death.

CHAPTER 6

Through all of this, I was reminded again of how strong my mother was. When I didn't think she would make it out of the hospital in October, she did—and here we were, three months later. Yet what little bit of fight she had left was about to be her last.

On Saturday, February 19, Austin and I went home to rest with the intention of going back to the nursing home in the morning. I had just fixed dinner when my phone rang. As I picked it up, the number appeared was the nursing home. I took a deep breath as I looked at Austin, telling him who it was after he asked. Even though I knew what I was about to hear, I was horrified. It was her nurse. She told me she had gone in to check on Mom, and she was already gone. I broke—I thought, *Gone? We were just there and now she's gone?* The nurse consoled me as much as she could on the phone and then asked if we wanted to come back, or did I just want them to call the funeral home. I couldn't even make that decision, so I asked her if I could call her back.

Austin embraced me, as we both fell to the floor in the den. With tears running down his cheeks, he said, "Mom, Mommaw is no longer in pain, and now she's with Papa." And how right he was. This is what she wanted. She was tired of the pain, tired of the fight...simply put, she was tired. When I told Austin the nurse

AND I DID...

asked if we wanted to come back in there, he piped up and said, "Yes, I want to go back." When I could not make a decision, my 11-year-old could.

I called Charlotte, and she and Ray, her husband, met us there. I also called my father's brother, my Uncle Charles, my first cousin Mike and his wife Melissa, as well as Preacher Jim and Judy. They too arrived shortly after we did. Walking in the room was daunting. This was the first time I had ever seen someone in this state, as I had chosen not to see my father when he passed. Of course, I couldn't help but regret the fact if we had stayed and not gone home earlier, we could have been there when she took her last breath. But then again, knowing my mother, she wouldn't have wanted anyone there...including Austin and me. So, maybe she had been waiting for us to leave.

Soon after we arrived and spoke with the nurse, they called the funeral home. Everyone stayed with us until she was taken away. Mom had fought a long, hard battle. Often you hear about those who lose their battles to cancer. I'd have to disagree in this case, as Mom won her battle. There is no doubt she met her Savior and was reunited with my father in heaven with no more cancer! No more chemo! No more radiation! No more neuropathy! No more pain! She could now walk without the assistance of a cane or walker! Praise God, praise God!

As we watched the funeral assistant take her away, it hit me just how tired and emotionally drained we were. The nurse kindly told me I could come back in the morning to get her things—and I did.

CHAPTER 7

Sunday morning, I drove to the nursing home listening to "Praise You in This Storm" over and over again. I found strength from the words of that song, as well as from my trust and faith in God. I reflected on the events of the last three months—in October, Mom had been in the hospital for an extended time, and then in November, we had moved her to assisted living. In December, we had moved her to the nursing home, and in January—January 19— she had passed. Through all of that I found peace in the fact I had done all I could do under the most difficult of circumstances. I was especially grateful to have had the support from Charlotte and other friends and family while managing to conjure up enough strength as an only child and single mom who had already lost her father.

As I arrived at the nursing home, I was greeted by lots of comforting hugs from the staff. One of them told me there was a nurse in Mom's room getting her things together for me. I thought about the day my father had passed...how I had to conjure up the strength to walk out of the hospital, carrying nothing but a bag of his personal belongings. Now here I was trying to summon up the strength to walk in Mom's room, where she no longer was, to gather up her personal things.

AND I DID...

When I walked through the door, I broke. I just sat down and cried. The nurse in the room consoled me and then told me she would give me some time alone. I immediately turned to God. I began to pray to God, seeking strength, wisdom, and peace of understanding of not just Mom's passing, but of the last several months...the last couple of years. When I lost my father, I cursed God. I was so mad at Him for taking my father, my rock, my mainstay. But this time, my emotions were much different. Thank God for His grace and forgiveness.

The nurse had several boxes for me to put Mom's things in. Although she had only been there about a month, there were several things to be packed up. Thank God, He gave me the strength to roll up my shirtsleeves and start packing. It didn't take as long as I thought it would. When I was finished, several nurses assisted in loading the boxes in my car. After one more round of hugs, I got in the car. As I was driving away, I looked in the rearview mirror, hoping to never return to this place.

I took the boxes by my parent's house. I unloaded the boxes one by one, putting them on the couch in the den where they would stay. I didn't know what to do with them—but more importantly, I didn't want to be in my mom and dad's cold, empty house any longer than I had to be. Far too many memories remained surreal. I would just relish the memories of Hee-Haw and popcorn at my own house.

CHAPTER 8

Although a few extended family members remained, I looked at Austin while we were making the funeral arrangements. He was sitting beside me, holding my hand. I was thinking, *Wow— it's just you and me now, but we will be OK*. Not only did I know we'd be OK, I promised my mother during her last time in the hospital we'd be OK. And no, I wasn't sure how, but I knew we would.

And Austin. He too has been through so much as a child...it breaks my heart. But much like me, he'd overcome these unbreakable moments—together—moments in life continue to define us. Yes, he is mature for his age, but unfortunately, he has had to grow up far too quickly.

As the funeral director continued to ask questions while we were making arrangements for my mother's visitation and funeral services, I thought back to the day, three years ago, when my mother was sitting across the same table from me. I was exhausted that day, but I had my mother, who was surprisingly sharp as a tack even after losing her husband, my father, very unexpectedly. I was at a loss for answers I should have been able to provide, while my mother answered almost everything as though it had all been rehearsed. Now, it was just me, and I was doing the best I could with the help of Charlotte, my Uncle Charles, Mike and Melissa, and Preacher Jim.

What I thought would have taken minutes at the funeral home took hours. I was so ready to leave and go home. Before we completed the arrangements, Austin asked if he could be excused to go the restroom. Surprisingly, he was gone forever before finally returning. But who could blame him? At the age of 11, Austin knew what it was like to lose those so close to him and to see those he loved suffer. He's a kid. How unfair, you know? *But don't question God's plan, Susan*, I told myself. Remember Proverbs 3:5-6. Are you familiar with that scripture?

Finally, all the information had been provided, and the decisions had been made. It was a cold Sunday afternoon, but it was a pretty day—unlike three years ago when we had lost my father and there had been how many inches of snow on the ground? And how many consecutive record-breaking days had there been with below-freezing temperatures?

Austin and I returned home to our family farm, to somber yet reassuring surroundings. As I made my way through the kitchen and dining room, I paused to look from my back door at the red brick house...on the hill, with a white fence surrounding it. Tears streamed down my face. It was all so different now. Even though my mother had not been there since October, she was no longer in an assisted-living facility, hospital, or nursing home. The house just looked so different to me, even from a distance.

Friends continued to drop by with food and to visit during the evening, showing their support, paying their respects, and expressing their condolences. During much of this time, Austin and I found ourselves cuddled up on the couch with one another. While reflecting on the events of the last twenty-four hours, I was reminded of Austin's unusually long absence while we were completing the funeral arrangements. So, I inquisitively asked him where he had gone when he disappeared this afternoon. He replied, "I met this guy, and he took me to his office and...." I responded with a smile, "Say no more." Austin is just like me. He never meets a stranger.

The next morning, I took Austin to school—he is such a trooper. Then I returned home to find myself sitting in total silence on my couch with a hot cup of coffee in hand. I was preparing to have my very own pity party, with no invited guests. Then, my phone rang. It was the women's center at my local hospital. I'd had my yearly mammogram last Thursday, and they needed me to return for more images, as there had been some changes in my right breast. I explained to them this was not a good time, as I had just lost my mother. Although sympathetic, the lady explained the radiologist liked to have patients return within a week of the initial mammogram. Since my mother's committal service was Wednesday, we made arrangements for Thursday, which would be one week to the day. I hung up the phone, not questioning God as to what else could happen, but simply asking Him to be with me because only He knew how much I can handle.

It didn't take long for me to forget about having to return to the women's center and to turn my thoughts to the loss of my mother. I didn't have time for nor did I want to do one of those videos to show during the visitation, but I did go through a bunch of pictures. I selected some for a collage we could display in the parlor, especially since my mother requested a closed casket. That was the one thing I'd heard my mom request since I was a child, "I want a closed casket when I die—I don't want people walking by gawking at me." If you knew my mother, I bet you just chuckled.

CHAPTER 9

Tuesday morning, I got up and threw on my sweats—literally. Not the cute fitted ones either, but the baggy fleece ones. Simply put? They were warmer. Oh, and I didn't make time for a shower. I wanted to do that when I returned home to get dressed for the visitation. I took Austin to school with the intention of picking him up in time to get him dressed and fed prior to the visitation beginning at 2 pm. The family was asked to be at the funeral home by 1 pm for the viewing before we closed the casket for the visitation. I know my cousin wanted to bet I'd be late, but I dare say no one took him up on it—they all know me too well. Sad to say, my dad would be very disappointed in me, as he'd always had a motto "If you can't be on time, be early." I'm sure that was the Marine in him. But I think he would forgive me and be proud of how I've coped as a single mom and only child—raising Austin, taking care of my mother, and managing a demanding, full-time job yet trying to keep God first in my life. I tried to keep my priorities a priority. Granted, there was very little and often no time for me, but that was OK—or at least I thought it was.

After I took Austin to school, I ran by the funeral home to practice the song I was going to play for my mother's funeral. My piano at home was so out of tune, plus some of the keys had begun to stick. Thank goodness, by the looks of the parking lot, there were not many people around. But for once—in my life—I honestly didn't care I looked like I had just rolled out of bed. When I walked in the front door, I was greeted by a few men whom I knew worked there, although there was one handsome gentleman I didn't recognize. I asked them if it was OK if I practiced my song a few times on their piano. One of the gentlemen took me back to the chapel and turned on the lights for me. I played the song maybe three or four times, as a few other staff members at the funeral home checked on me to see if I needed anything. I was thinking, *Coffee and a shower?* But I'd be home shortly to take care of both.

After returning home and giving very little thought to what I would wear to kick-off my day, I began giving more well-planned thought to what I was going to wear for the visitation and funeral, which were being held in the afternoon and evening. Between phone calls and a few friends and neighbors stopping by, I suddenly found myself in a tizzy, trying to get ready while allowing enough time to grab some chicken nuggets for Austin prior to picking him up at school and giving him ample time to eat and change. With nuggets in one hand and his clothes in the other, we arrived just a few minutes after 1 pm. My cousin had that smirky grin on his face as we came barreling through the front door of the funeral home to find everyone else there. I looked at him and said, "Don't say a word," as I smiled back at him seconds later in a lighthearted way.

The first visitation was held from 2 to 4 pm, followed by another visitation from 6 to 8 pm, with the funeral service at 8 pm. Fortunately, the funeral home provided us—the family—with a catered meal between the visitations. While downstairs trying to rest my feet and legs for a bit, as I had chosen to not use my cane, and enjoy a bite to eat, I realized I had left my phone upstairs, in the parlor—in my purse. My purse! I didn't remember what was in it, but it didn't matter. When a woman is separated from her purse it's like—well, I don't know what it's like—but I hurried upstairs to get it. And there it was—right where I had left it in the parlor, but my phone was not in my purse. I panicked. Under normal circumstances, I probably could have handled a missing phone, but not this time. I went back downstairs, thinking, *Maybe I carried it down here and just don't remember.* Wrong. As my tailspin continued, I stopped and decided to retrace my steps, beginning in my car. In the meantime, Austin found the man whom he had befriended on Sunday. Together they too began combing the funeral home, looking for my phone. As one step led to another, there it was—where I had left it...in the pocket of my coat, which was hanging in the coat closet. As I was walking down the hall, very relieved, I ran into Austin and his newfound friend, who was a funeral director, and I thanked the gentleman for helping us look for my phone. Did I mention how good-looking he was?

Many friends and family members attended the visitations as well as the funeral service. As I did for my father's funeral, I delivered the eulogy after playing my mother one last song on the piano, "We Shall Behold Him." It was a beautiful service...what a tribute to her and to my father. Our family has truly been blessed with many friends. Following the events of the evening, a few of my girlfriends came over with lots of Mexican takeout, and we talked, and I cried...and we talked, and I cried some more.

The next day, we prepared for the conclusion of the funeral, the graveside service. We met at the funeral home before proceeding to the cemetery. It was a beautiful day but very chilly. Despite the eloquent words spoken during the funeral the evening before and during the committal service, and no matter how kind friends were in showing their care and concern, there was still a very real, genuine, and valid sense of sorrow...a loss that is experienced when a loved one is no longer with us.

Following the brief remarks and prayer at the funeral home, Austin and I got in my car. I drove to the cemetery, just as I had done when my father passed away. But this time, instead of my mother riding in the passenger seat, there sat Austin. "*Here we go again,*" I thought. Although tears ran down our faces as I drove with my left hand, my right hand clinched with Austin's hand, we both knew my mother was so much better off and, more importantly, she was reunited with my father, for whom she had grieved since the day he passed. So why was this so hard? Why did it hurt so much?

At the conclusion of the graveside service, we made our way to the church, where a meal had been prepared for everyone. I tried to eat, but the events of the last few days were catching up with me. The potted plants and flowers had been delivered from the funeral home to the church where we, the family, could disseminate them. Again, I found myself so ready to leave, but there were things that had to be done, and I was the one in charge.

Even after we had distributed many of the plants and novelties to family and friends, we loaded up my car with the remaining plants...more than I knew what to do with. My car actually looked like a florist's vehicle on their busiest day of the year! But Austin and I made our way home and unloaded them. Then we decided to go back to the cemetery and see the grave after all the beautiful flowers had been placed. Given the freezing temperatures, we knew they would not last long. I took a few pictures, then Austin and I began to pick some to make our own bouquet arrangements so we could enjoy them at home. After returning home, surprisingly, Austin wanted to go back and get some more! And we did—before settling in for the evening.

CHAPTER 10

As the day was coming to an end, despite all I had been through the last several days, I was suddenly reminded of my mammogram tomorrow…ugh. Thank goodness one of my friends, Jamila, had already told me she was going with me—no ifs, ands, or buts.

I picked her up at work then we headed to the women's center for my appointment. As my name was called, we walked back together. I was asked to remove my shirt and put on a top-like gown. After I was taken in for one image on my right breast, I was asked to be seated as the radiologist would read it to determine if more images were needed.

We waited for what seemed like forever. Then, I was asked to come in another room for another image. Again, I was asked to be seated and wait for the radiologist to review those images. After what was probably only a few minutes, yet, felt like eternity, I was then told the radiologist wanted to have an ultrasound completed—really???

I have to admit, by this time I was getting somewhat anxious, so I was thrilled Jamila was with me to console me. Following the ultrasound, the radiologist came in the room while I was still lying on the table. He told me despite how hard he had tried to find something, he couldn't. He did want me to come back in six months, which would be around June or July, for a follow-up.

Wow...what a sigh of relief. I was very thankful to God, as I had no idea how I would've handled any other difficult news at that time.

CHAPTER 11

Funny how life has a way of moving on despite the obstacles we are faced with. There are so many times in life when I've wanted to blow the whistle, call time out, and either regroup or let time stand still until I could catch my breath.

Since life doesn't wait, many times I have thanked God for Austin, as he has a way of helping me move on. Given the many distractions that came with my job, Austin's homework, school activities, basketball, etc., it didn't take long before I found myself marching to the drum of life once again. But I won't lie...there were several days I would've given anything to stay in bed and pull the covers over my head, shutting out everyone and everything.

Since September 2012 when I suffered a stroke, yes, a stroke, I have had several heart-to-hearts with God. After questioning *Why?* when God took Dad, I no longer question *why* I have been through so much. Instead, I ask *How?*...how can I take my trial and bring glory to Him? But I have to admit, after losing my mother, I was hoping my journey in life was going to be free of some challenges for a while. Speaking of my stroke, or rather my "event," plus all the stress of the New Year, getting back in my groove at work, then within a few weeks losing my mother, I found myself at a breaking point. But it's coming now? After the fact? I thought

I was strong! I thought I had handled everything really well...why now? What is going on with me?

Several weeks after returning to work after losing my mother, I was traveling back from a work-related event. I felt so sick—nauseously sick—plus I hurt all over. It was so difficult to concentrate, no matter how hard I tried. I had already decided upon my return to work I was going home and going to bed. My world around me felt like it was all crashing in. *What's happening to me?* I thought. Upon my return, I got in my car, started it, and just sat there for a few minutes, breaking down in tears. So, I decided to call my doctor just to see if he possibly had any appointments though it was doubtful since it was late in the day. When his receptionist answered then checked his schedule, she said, "Can you be here in 10 minutes?" I said, "Yes. I'm on my way."

After about five minutes, if that long, into my examination, my doctor quickly diagnosed me. No, it was not a cold or the flu. It was depression. *What??? No way!!! Depression???* "I can't be depressed," I proclaimed. The few life-changing events I had encountered were over—they were done. I was moving on with life. Well, my doctor quickly told me people like me, who are strong, often do not experience the emotions related to, say, a stroke or losing a loved one until after the events. Then he reminded me I could probably add the loss of my father to that list, which had happened only three years ago...it had all caught up with me. He wrote me a prescription and wanted to see me back in a few weeks. I picked up Austin from school after my appointment, with a smile on my face, determined to beat my depression—on my own—and not let anyone know!

But when I left the doctor's office, I left with a feeling of defeat, as well as one of somewhat embarrassment and shame. Me? The strong one? How did I let the events in my life get to me so badly I was now dealing with depression? How was I going to tell people what was wrong? I'd have given anything to call work and

AND I DID...

tell them I had the flu. But that was not the case—I had to come to grips with my depression. So, OK, here it goes...my name is Susan Crum, and I have depression. There. I said it. I admitted it. And you know what? It was OK. I began taking my prescription. At first I thought it made me feel better, but within a few weeks my stomach began hurting very badly—yep, from the medicine. I was getting ready to go out of town on a business trip, so I contacted my doctor. He suggested I hold off on the medicine until I returned. Despite the fact it seemed to be helping, that's exactly what I did. Although I was a bit concerned...I didn't want to find myself in the same mental state I had been in only a short while ago.

But since my doctor suggested I not take my medicine, it was one more opportunity to lean on God—maybe more than ever. My business trip went well. It was the first time I had traveled overnight since my stroke and since losing my mother. I found myself picking up the phone to call her as I always did when I traveled to let her know I had arrived safely or just to touch base. I'd look at my phone. Look away. Smile and move on.

Following my trip, I never took another pill for depression. I'm so thankful I didn't wait until it was too late to seek God. Instead, I chose to walk with Him in the midst of it. And as a result, I'll be the first to admit, I am a very fortunate one. Millions of Americans fight this disease every day, but no one should feel like a failure if prescription medication is needed. Depression is an illness just like diabetes or any other. It is not always within our control. But with God's help, I was determined to beat my depression, too—just like I beat my stroke. But did I?

CHAPTER 12

Chapters 11 and 12. These may be the hardest chapters I've ever written, yet I feel compelled to share one of my darkest secrets—my battle with depression. But in sharing this experience with readers, I pray God will use my experience to help others in what feel like impossible situations. If this can help one person—just one—then praise God for giving me the courage to share.

As you read in Chapter 11, it was so difficult for me to admit I suffered from depression. For me? It was so embarrassing. It felt like it was a sign of weakness. But I'm not weak! I'm Superwoman! I can handle anything and everything life throws at me...I can't be fighting depression. Yeah, right. First and foremost, depression is *not* a weakness of character. Being positive doesn't mean always telling everyone you're OK when you're not. To be positive, you also have to be a realist. You have to be in touch with your emotions and, more importantly, express them when appropriate. Life is not always going to be a sailboat on a calm sea. And acceptance of this? It begins at the heart.

Feeling down is a normal part of life. How many times in life have we felt down and out? Has someone let you down in life? Have things not gone as planned? Have you too lost loved ones? Have your dreams been crushed? If you've answered yes to any of these questions, you've experienced sadness...probably a sadness beyond any feeling words could describe. But if your sadness fails to pass, if you don't bounce back, if you refuse to interact with people or enjoy life, you certainly could be experiencing some form of depression, as I did. Does this describe you? If so, please seek help. Turn to God. Do not reject the One who really loves you, the One who is your Hope, and your Life, the One who is your source of Joy. David wrote about his depression, *"Why am I discouraged? Why so sad? I will put my hope in God! I will praise him again—my Savior and my God!"* (Psalms 43:5 NLT)

Please don't be like I was and suppress your feelings, thinking they're normal or they will just go away. Are you concerned for a loved one who may be suffering from depression? Then ensure they receive help. Depression is real...very real. Lift them up and call on God during this time. We must live for God to become fully equipped with the right "spiritual armor" needed for this kind of battle. Remember, when we fear God, we cannot fear man or anything else that exists in the world.

Did you know 350 million people battle depression across the world? So please know you are *not* the only one feeling isolated! So you're not one in a million—you're one of 350 million! You are *not* the only one feeling withdrawn from your family and friends! You are *not* the only one feeling helpless! You are *not* the only one feeling worthless! You are *not* the only one feeling alone or rejected! You are *not* the only one crying for no reason! You are *not* the only one suffering from overwhelming sadness!

Please know depression is one battle you don't have to fight alone. Yet, I know how difficult it was for me to reach out to someone— anyone—who I could trust and talk to about my feelings. I found it very difficult to share my thoughts, feelings, and emotions because of inhibitions and my innermost fears. I fought feelings of hopelessness and helplessness. So what happened? All of that became bottled up inside of me until my internal gauge was past full. Have you ever set the thing-a-ma-jig on the gas nozzle to walk away or get in your car...and then realize gas is gushing out everywhere (you knew I couldn't write a book without mentioning gas)? My thoughts about all my recent adversities were gushing out of my mind...out of control...chasing each other round and round. There was no peace of mind. Little did I know they were manifesting into depression.

As with me, early detection is key. Acceptance is equally important. And knowing you can overcome depression is imperative. No matter how strong we think we are, we must realize and accept the fact there are times and phases in our lives when we will experience serious difficulties—but these points are not the end of the road.

Yes, depression can feel never-ending, especially when the exhaustion takes over and everything—*everything*—seems incredibly hard. That is especially important to recognize, as we all need to view our recovery as being accomplished step by step, not in one giant leap. Reflect on what is normal in your daily routines...and do it! Don't let depression rob you of the things you enjoy most in life, like your family, friends, hobbies, etc. As hard as it can be, keep your focus on the good things in life and your outlook positive. And don't forget—you can control your thoughts! Remember, we may not choose our adversities in life, but we have a choice about how we respond to them. Avoiding negative and unpleasant conversations or situations simply takes a conscious decision.

Based on my experience, one of the best things helped me beat my depression was distractions. Like work. Remember the business trip I made shortly after being diagnosed? That was one of the best things I could have done. It was a reminder life moves on. At this conference, I saw many people I only see once a year. Many of them knew about my recent adversities, but their words of encouragement were a reminder life does move on. I even danced for the first time since my stroke! It felt great...I felt alive once again! I can't often control my hardships, but I can control how I respond—and I did.

And of course, there's Austin—thank God for him. He's an easy distraction for me, with his jokes (even when they don't make sense to me), his dimples, his smile, his favorite book, homework, basketball practice, ball games...the list goes on and on.

I also turned to my friends, my network of support. My hobbies, such as golf, exercise. Whatever is in your life that creates positivity should be one of the first places you turn. But the very first place I should have turned—and so should you—was God. Yes, I prayed and told myself I trusted Him and His plan—but did I really? Were those just words? I soon recognized my faith was not as strong as it should have been. And after all I'd gone through, you would think it would be, right? Yeah, me too. I was so emotionally distraught...but once I chose to turn my eyes on Him, truly trusting, believing all of this unexplainable happenings in my life were part of His plan, I felt a healing...a healing of my depression.

So, I encourage you to try your best to not dwell on unfortunate experiences, corrupt news in the world today (seriously, limit your news watching to 20 minutes a day), or ways in which life seems to have cheated your plans and dreams. Instead, think about all the ways life has been a blessing to you, and keep your eyes on God—at all times. I told someone recently despite all the adversities in my life, my blessings far outweigh my difficulties. The abundant life, which only God can give us, prepares our hearts with a mature love to endure pain and suffering. The apostle Paul says *this mature love bears all things, believes all things, hopes all things, endures all things. Love never fails* (1 Corinthians 13:7-8). Know God created you in His image—therefore you are good. He wants you to be happy, but He understands us when we're not.

Today, I choose to not be a helpless victim of depression. Recovering from depression, for most, can be a long and difficult journey. If you have suffered from depression like I did, I pray we do not relapse. By offering positive energy and thoughts to others, I choose—and yes, it is my choice—to live each day to its fullest. When something negative enters your mind, immediately replace it with a positive, something good. I encourage you to live life one day at a time. And most importantly, seek God's spirit in order for Him to lead and rule your life.

CHAPTER 13

During a three-year period, I overcame several adversities, yet during that time I developed the foundation for the closest relationship with Christ I ever thought imaginable. It is a relationship, until now, I've only heard others talk about. I knew I was a believer...a child of God...but something was missing. I'd heard other Christians talk about their faith and trust and thought mine was strong, yet their walk with Christ seemed different. But why? I began to reflect...when adversity would come my way, whether it was big or small, most of the time I'd take it all on my own. Eventually I'd turn to God, searching for the path in which to rely upon my faith and trust in Him—but it was so weak. It was often hard to find.

To that end, I've made it a point to strengthen my daily walk with Christ. Maybe like you, I've never liked the thought of calling on Him just when I needed Him or when I heard the storm winds of life begin to howl. But honestly, those seemed to be the times I called on Him the most. How many times did I pause and simply thank Him for all of his many blessings, His grace, His forgiveness, etc.? I could go on and on!

Do you have children? If so, think about it. What if your child only called on you when he or she needed something? If they never

AND I DID...

paused to say "Thank you" or to sit quietly in your presence? How would you feel? What kind of relationship would that be?

When I started earnestly seeking God's favor every day of my life and not first praying for my needs, but first thanking Him—thanking Him for His goodness and his many blessings—my ability to trust and put my faith in Him changed. In addition, I began asking Him to equip me for *works of service, so that the body of Christ may be built up* (Ephesians 4:12).

A daily walk with Christ should be part of our daily lives, despite what may come our way. In case you're wondering, I'll tell you why. If we strengthen our relationship with Him every day, no matter the circumstances, when adversities meet us face to face, we are already in His presence—we don't have to stop and call on Him. We're already praying with Him, talking with Him, sharing our day with Him. Growing spiritually doesn't come as a result of adversity. Growing spiritually comes as a result of using those adversities to glorify God, focusing on the purpose and plan He has for our lives. We must truly accept Romans 8:28—*We know that all things work together for good to them that love God, to them who are called according to His purpose.*

Once you believe this verse—truly believe this verse—pray God will open your eyes to lessons you can learn through adversities and doors of opportunities to encourage others. There is such a difference in reacting with our emotions as opposed to spiritually when adversities come our way. I've heard this quote many times: "Your outlook *will* determine your outcome." Our outlook on adversity must be one of glorifying Christ through any and all situations, and then sharing Him and your testimony with others. Remember, we often want God to change our circumstances. We pray, "God please give me a new job, more money,...." But don't forget, God wants to use our circumstances to change us...yes, even the most challenging ones, too.

CHAPTER 14

One of my favorite times of the day came around 5:30 am during the workweek. Yes, in the morning. That was when—most mornings—I would bounce out of bed and jump on the treadmill for a thirty-minute walk with weights in hand. And—most mornings—I'd also try to work in some toning exercises. No, it wasn't always easy to get up that early, but I had a friend tell me once it's "mind over mattress," and how true that is!

It was the fall of 2012. Austin had decided he was going to enter the draft to play football. I managed to get him there after we realized the draft was upon us. As we arrived, I had no idea what to expect. I assumed he would run, throw the football, etc. Once the draft got underway, his age group was asked to move to a particular part of the gym. There were only about eight of them. *But doesn't it take more than eight to make a team???* As this was a learning experience for me, I found out if you played last year in this league, you did not have to go through the draft again.

So there they stood, each holding up a number in front of himself...like criminals...with about five or six men talking among themselves. It wasn't long before Austin's number was called. The man, who would be his coach, called him over, informing Austin he would be on the Eagles' team.

AND I DID...

Even though I had been a cheerleader in high school, it was amazing how little I knew about football. And now, many years later, I still realize how little I know, but I'm still Austin's biggest fan and looked forward to our first season of football.

CHAPTER 15

On September 18, 2012, I did not bounce out of bed at 5:30 am for my ritual morning workout, but after we returned home that evening, I made time to get it in...well, part of it. Austin was leaving the next day for an overnight school trip to the 4-H camp. We had packed most of his things in preparation for his trip. Homework was complete. Dinner was consumed. I was going to hit the treadmill for at least 30 minutes and make up for the workout I missed earlier that morning.

I had been incorporating a walk with weights in hand plus jogging. I had finally worked my way up to walking half a mile, then running three miles, and cooling down by walking another half a mile, for a total of four miles. I wanted to begin running 5Ks in the spring.

So, I hopped on the treadmill, making my way to a fast-paced trot with my weights in hand—a two-for-one workout. Can't beat that, right? Well, shortly after this trek began, my world changed.

CHAPTER 16

I remember thinking, *I wish Austin would quit pushing on my stomach.* It hurt, but I couldn't move or open my eyes or speak. I could sense his panic, his tears, his fear.

I remember a man's voice saying, "She didn't even respond" and "Get the kid out of here." I was so scared. What was happening?

Finally, I began to come to in the ambulance. One of the paramedics told me we were stopping at the nearest hospital, which is not the one I would normally use. But I felt so helpless. I nodded my consent, as I found it difficult to speak. Probably from passing out, right?

"Austin! Where's Austin?" I was able to get his name out, and the paramedic told me he was with Preacher Jim and Judy, and they were behind us. I wondered how in the world he got with them, but it didn't matter. Thank God he was with them.

Then I thought about Mom. She was not going to handle this well and—bless her heart again—there is little she could do. I knew that was so hard on her, as she had shared with me time and time again—usually accompanied by tears—how she wished she could help me at home, pick up or take Austin, etc. But given her health, she could barely take care of herself.

When we arrived in the emergency room, the doctor quickly examined me and he was confident I'd had a stroke. Austin was by my side, tears streaming down his face. I'll never forget the look of fear on his precious face. I repeatedly told him "I'm O...K... I'm O...K" Those were about the easiest words I could get out of my mouth. Within a short period of time, I was back in the ambulance headed to a hospital in Bristol, which is considered the stroke center in our region.

So much of that evening is a blur. My cousin Mike and his wife Melissa were in the ER, and then they followed us to Bristol. However, I think he took the scenic route as it seemed like it took them forever to get there. I thought Austin was riding with them to Bristol, but when they arrived my cousin told me Austin had decided to go home with Preacher Jim and Judy. He just couldn't handle it. I knew he was a nervous wreck, but I just wanted to hold him and assure him I was going to be OK...I'd be fine tomorrow.

Austin, my 11-year-old son, is now my hero. Austin heard me collapse. I imagine the sound of the weights hitting the treadmill on the floor made a terribly loud noise. When he got to me, he tried to use my phone to call 911, but he was so petrified he apparently could not remember the passcode. But he did remember there was a button on our alarm system, when selected, went directly to 911. So he pushed it.

My phone rang, but it was a number Austin didn't know, so he didn't answer it. Then the number called again. This time Austin answered even though I had always told him not to answer a number he didn't know. It was the 911 office. He explained to them what had happened, and of course, the ambulance was already on its way. Once he told me this, I was so proud of him. He probably saved my life by responding as quickly as he did under an inordinate amount of stress and emotion.

CHAPTER 17

It was ironic I was rushed to Bristol for an MRI, as no one there seemed to possess a sense of urgency. We arrived around midnight, and nurses would pop in and check on me, but that was about it. I do remember it was about 9:30 pm that evening before I had an MRI. I thought the whole point of rushing me there was to have an MRI to detect whether or not I'd had a stroke.

But during the early morning hours, I realized I could not move my right arm or my right leg and I could only say a few words even though I knew what I wanted to say...it was so frustrating and even scarier. As the new day dawned, a speech therapist, occupational therapist, and physical therapist evaluated my condition. Each one began working with me in their own area, with little to no improvement. I was thinking, *Can they not fix this...like now? I need to get home to Austin and my mom!*

Surprisingly, I had several visitors the following day, including my mom. Yes, my mom! The hospital is at least an hour away, but she wanted to come see me, so Preacher Jim and Judy brought her to the hospital. Here she came, being wheeled into my room in a wheelchair. Mom detested wheelchairs, but in this case, this was her only option if she wanted to see her daughter.

I could barely get any words out of my mouth, yet I knew what I wanted to say. My right side was completely useless. I had to drag my leg while using a walker. My hand wouldn't stay on top of the walker. Unbelievable! *This has got to be better in a few hours*, I thought to myself.

I was so scared. I wanted to be with Austin. I wanted to go home and resume the workout I hadn't completed the night before. I wanted my life back. I wanted to be able to get out of bed and walk out of there and to speak all the words lingering in my brain but would not come out. I wanted to be able to take a shower without one of my girlfriends having to assist me.

Yet I assured my mom and others I was OK, because I knew I'd be OK—hopefully within the next day or so. I honestly didn't know how and when, but I did know I had too much to live for. I was 42 years old, and I had to take care of Austin and my mom. I had to be able to speak, walk, write, feed myself, and do all the things I'm accustomed to doing. There was no way this was a dream, because it was as real as real could be.

CHAPTER 18

I really liked my speech therapist. Ironically, she too had suffered a stroke a few years ago—in the parking lot of the hospital! She reminded me of a drill sergeant. Although I have no idea what a drill sergeant is like, I was convinced she could be one! She pushed me—she pushed me hard. She would make me pat my hand, my left hand, on my lap or the table to every syllable of every word I was trying to speak...aaaaaaargh! It was so frustrating! I knew what I wanted to say—I just couldn't get it out. Nonetheless, she and I had a connection. She would often come by my room to just check on me, not to drill me with words. I can still hear her heels clicking down the hall. I always heard her before I saw her. She also was involved as a volunteer with a few area non-profit organizations, so her sense of philanthropy also resonated with me. At the time I had no idea, but meeting my speech therapist was certainly a "Godwink."

She even made a special trip to her car to get me a book—which, by the way, I still have. Oops! Apparently the book had accompanied her on a recent trip to the beach, as it smelled of suntan oil. What I would have given at that moment to be lying on the beach—not in a hospital bed— reading this book! But the book provided a turning point for me. It was titled "Divine Alignment:

How Godwinks Guide Your Journey." If you have read my blog on my website, you will see a blog about Godwinks.

I've always been the type of person who didn't at all times believe things were just coincidental. I believed God's hand was in it, but I had never coined a phrase for this or known how to best describe it. But SQuire (yes the Q is capitalized) Rushnell, the author of the book, beautifully defines those times as Godwinks. I looooove that term!

Here I am, an hour away from home, scared, not knowing what has happened or what's going to happen or when it's going to happen. But maybe none of this is coincidental...it is God's plan, a Godwink in my life. He's going to use this. I don't know why or how, but He is.

CHAPTER 19

After I had the MRI that night, the doctor told me there was no indication I had had a stroke. So basically, there was nothing they could do. However, they were going to run a few more tests in an effort to obtain a diagnosis. From that point forward, the doctors referred to my no-stroke as an "event." So, to this day, we often refer to it as my "event," even using our fingers for the quotes.

Thank God, the next day, on Thursday, my dear friend Debbie came to see me and spent the day with me. Her husband had suffered a massive stroke several years ago, so she was well-attuned to my situation. It was so comforting to have her with me. It's like she just knew what to do, what to say, what questions to ask.

The therapists continued to visit me that day and do what I considered to be little things. I guess it was enough therapy to say they did something, because I certainly wasn't any better. And why wasn't I getting better? I was not impressed with my progress, but I did come to like the occupational therapist, too. She'd had a family member suffer a stroke, which influenced her decision to pursue a career as an OT.

Since, according to them, I hadn't had a stroke, I was scheduled to be discharged the next day, Friday. But where was I going to go? I couldn't walk without using a walker, dragging my right leg behind or raise my right hand or arm or even speak! What was I going to do? They recommended three outpatient clinics—none of which was in Greeneville. Before Debbie left, she told me she would be back the next day to take me home and I was not to worry...we'd figure it all out.

In the meantime, my best friend, Donna, who lives in Kentucky, called. She told me she was coming to stay with me that weekend. What a blessing and a Godwink moment. How selfless of her to leave her twin daughters and husband to come home and take care of me for the weekend.

When Friday came, we continued to get mixed messages about my therapy. I'm thankful Debbie was there. I was an emotional wreck. They told me since I didn't have a stroke, I would not qualify for inpatient rehab, which was what we wanted because I needed to get better as soon as possible. I was 42—not 82—years old, with a son and a mother to take care of and a demanding job I couldn't part with. So upon being discharged, I left with orders for therapy three days a week for one hour a day at a local hospital. I thought, *At this pace, I'll be better—when?* I was so scared.

CHAPTER 20

Debbie stayed with me until Donna arrived Friday evening. By the way, these two friends were simply incredible. Debbie was making plans for friends to stay with me around the clock after Donna left on Sunday, as I could obviously not stay alone. She was also making arrangements for friends to bring food.

The outpouring of support that weekend was incredible. Austin was with his dad, but he came to visit me on Sunday as he was going to stay with a paternal uncle and aunt who lived across town. She was a teacher, which was a plus, as I knew Austin would need help with his homework. Despite my physical incapacities, being away from Austin was the hardest part of all. The fact I could not speak or walk or do any of the day-to-day rituals I was accustomed to was nothing in comparison to the ache in my heart.

Friends and family continued to drop by bringing food, flowers, and smiles of encouragement. Although I am a very positive person, this was a situation where I had to look long and hard for the good. But I was alive, I had Austin—although he was not with me at the time—I had my mom, and I was blessed with a plethora of friends.

Ironically, my two first cousins, Mike and Alan, were both at my house on Sunday. Unfortunately, we don't get together enough. Under the command of Debbie and Donna, they helped move furniture, making a pathway for me and my walker from the couch in the den to my bedroom that hopefully would not trip me up.

Another friend, Lisa, came over to mow the yard. As she said, even though it's Sunday, "If the cow's in the ditch, we've got to get her out!" And the way she saw it, the cow was in the ditch.

Around mid-afternoon on Sunday, it was time for Donna to head home. I could never thank her enough for everything she did for me that weekend. I cried when she left, as though it would be the last time I'd ever see her.

CHAPTER 21

Although I had orders for outpatient rehab beginning the upcoming week, on Monday some of my closest friends reached out to another local hospital that had an inpatient rehab unit. After reviewing my reports from Bristol, they said they would take me as a patient whether I had had a stroke or not. What an answer to prayer! I would be receiving a minimum of three hours of therapy a day. Now that was more like it! Maybe I would get better and resume my life in a few weeks.

On Tuesday morning, a representative from the hospital even came to my house to complete all the necessary paperwork for admittance. Friends helped pack my suitcase, as I was leaving on a journey to get my life back. All of it! And I wasn't coming home without it!

Wednesday morning, my mother came down to see me before I left. She had made a few trips down to see me, as I lived below her on the family farm. I've said it before—I moved from one end of the farm to the other. And—bless her heart once more—she would sit and just rub my right hand, although I know her hands hurt so badly with her arthritis and neuropathy. She'd even talk to my hand, telling it to move and to "Wake up!" Those were precious moments I'll never forget. Besides, nobody can rub a child like a mother can.

When Debbie pulled in my driveway, I knew it was time. It was time to leave my house and move into a rehab unit. *None of this makes sense,* I thought many times to myself. But this seemed to be the only way. I'd work hard to get better and be home soon. I was determined to get better—quickly. One of my friends and neighbors, David, was there helping me get out of the house. As I was trying to navigate the walker through the doorway and down the steps, he suddenly scooped me up in his arms and carried me to Debbie's car, placing me gently in the passenger seat. I told him, "Thank you," although I knew I could have managed.

Upon our arrival at the hospital, Debbie's husband, Mike, was there to greet us. He wheeled me up to the rehab unit and to my room. Wow—it was huge! It had apparently been a double room, but now it only had one bed but two TVs. Sounds exciting, right? Uhm, not so much. There I sat in the recliner, helpless as Debbie scurried around the room putting up my things while I asked myself, *Can I really do this? Maybe she should just take me back home.*

It wasn't long before the doctor, who was the director of the inpatient rehab unit, came in. After her evaluation, she told me, "It looks like a stroke, walks like a stroke, so we're going to treat it as a stroke." Following her evaluation, the physical therapist, John, came in to conduct his assessment. He was followed by the occupational therapist, Oyden, who was then followed by the speech therapist, Jamila. The doctor, in addition to the therapists, asked me what my goal was. Not being familiar with strokes, I sat up in the chair, and I was able to say, "Two...weeks." Aggressive? Maybe...but that was my goal.

At the time, I was the only patient in the unit, so I received a lot of attention the first few days. I even got to enjoy lunch in my room, as opposed to the dining room, where all the rehab patients were asked to come together for lunch. The first time I had to do that, I was so intimidated. I think the average age in the unit was 70. So, making my way on my walker into a room of three or four other patients—one at each table and who also were there to overcome some therapeutic deficiencies—made me very uncomfortable. There was no conversation. *Could they not talk either?* Then after we ate, we would wait until someone was available to take us back to our room, as most of us were in a wheelchair or using a walker. You know what the best part of lunch was? Going back to your room.

The administration had originally told me they preferred visitors come by after 4 pm but they were pretty lenient—or so they said. Well, after about the third day, a sign was put on my door, indicating I was in therapy Monday-Friday from 8 am to 4 pm—no visitors during this time. Well, Debbie and I both knew this did not apply to her, as she came every day at lunch. She would pick up my dirty clothes and bring clean ones she had washed at her house. All of the therapists were fine with her in the room if it was during a session. She would crawl up in the big chair and never made a peep. She may have shed a tear, but she rarely made a sound. Most days she would even come back late in the afternoon. It didn't take me long to realize she was determined to not let me fall into depression. Having gone through something similar—but on a greater scale—with her husband, she knew how easy it would be and it would probably happen to me, even though I assured her it would not.

CHAPTER 22

A few days later, my physical therapist took me to the gym for the first time. As I made my way in, I noticed the mirrors on the wall. I immediately turned away. I did not want to see myself this way. However, he was putting me on the bars, which meant I'd be walking toward the mirrors. Ugh—I felt a knot in my stomach. *Damn it, Susan, get it together. You can do this*, I told myself.

For my first time, I did pretty well. I was determined to walk again, and this was part of my recovery. But it was so hard to look at myself in the mirrors. I hated it. I did.

Around lunchtime, I was sitting in my room when Debbie came blowing in. She pulled up a chair in front of me, held my hands, and asked me what was wrong. She knew within seconds upon entering the room something was bothering me, although I tried to hide it. Tears streamed down my face as I tried to tell her I saw myself in the mirror for the first time. She held me, cried with me, and in her incredible way, spoke words to me that lifted me up and put everything in perspective. And then she wheeled me to the dining room for lunch. That's Debbie!

CHAPTER 23

My goal of making a complete recovery in two weeks was not achieved. Everyone knew it probably wouldn't be—well, everyone but me. But it wasn't for lack of effort...I tried. I tried hard...I really did. Regardless, I was making the most progress with my right hand and arm. Even before I regained the slightest use of my right hand, I managed to type a blog on my website with only my left hand. Now that was an accomplishment! And yes, I was disappointed I did not attain my goal, but I did not let that deter me from continuing to give it my best! Every day, it was speech, occupational therapy, and physical therapy—and sometimes PT twice a day! And every day, things that had been being done for me were gradually not being done, as a way to push me.

I remember the day my OT came in the room and stripped my bed. As much as I liked her, I wanted to curse her—I really did. But I made the bed as well as I could. And this daily routine took me how long? I was exhausted. And do you know what she did after I made it? She stripped it again. And yes, I made it a second time.

It wasn't long before the PT had me in the stairwell, going up and down the stairs. And walking, walking, walking the halls.

How many words did I have to say 20 times each? In addition, my speech therapist made me sing songs, like "Happy Birthday."

And since one part of my job was speaking, she had an idea for me to write a letter to someone, which I would read to him or her once I had progressed with my speech and, of course, had completed the letter. Which do you think came first? Anyway, I didn't have to think about it long. Who was the first person who came to mind? Debbie.

CHAPTER 24

It was almost a month after I was admitted to the rehab unit, and I had made good progress, but I was still not at 100% yet. At this point, however, I decided it was time for me to be discharged. And the great thing? All of the therapists—and the doctor—agreed with me. But I had to be discharged with 24/7 care, as I was not yet capable of being alone—this was primarily for my own safety. Thank God for a friend who made arrangements for a local organization to provide care for me so I could go home.

Yes, I was scared. I had grown close to several of the nurses and staff members. If only they could all go home with me. There had been many Godwinks during my time there. One of the housekeepers, after cleaning my room one day, came back, asking me if she could share something with me. She and her husband survived the devastating tornados that had, surprisingly, hit our community in 2011, taking several lives. I was so touched by her story. What an inspiration she was.

One evening a nurse came in and brought me a scripture. She was a single mom. We connected so well. I just hated she worked the night shift...I thankfully slept most of the nights, so I didn't get to see her as often as I would have liked. Another nurse, who shares my first name, asked me one night if she could pray with me. After that night, every night she worked, we prayed. Had I not had my "event," I doubt I would have experienced these Godwinks...among others.

CHAPTER 25

The week after I was discharged, Debbie, Austin, and one of my caregivers took me to a doctor in Knoxville for a second opinion. We were up before the sun, as my appointment was first thing in the morning. The doctor performed a pretty thorough exam and reviewed my records. He then wanted me to come back for several tests in a few days, so we made the appointment. But before we left, he ordered an inordinate amount of blood work–like 12 or 14 vials. And yes, I almost passed out when I stood up. So embarrassing.

By the time we got to the car, I was not feeling well, but we all agreed I just needed food. So we stopped on our way home for lunch. I didn't eat very much, as it all was making me feel worse and not better. And on the way home, something happened. I don't remember a lot of the details, but according to Debbie, I passed out, and they could not get me to come to. After Debbie called my doctor, who told her he'd meet us at the ER, she said she was holding Austin with one arm and reaching her other arm between the seats, holding onto me while our caregiver was driving like Mario Andretti to get us to the hospital.

After my examination in the ER, I was admitted. "Has she had another stroke?" "All of the progress she has made, is it gone?"

Everyone was very concerned. Yet my doctor was convinced it was not a relapse. Everyone prayed he was right.

Given the uncertainty of my condition and recovery, Austin's father and I decided it was best if he lived with them, which was about an hour away, while I continued to focus on my recovery. He would go to school there and stay with me on the weekends. But praise be to God, what could have been months only lasted three weeks before Austin returned home and to his own school. Again, what an overcomer Austin is—he got along exceptionally well at the other school. He made friends quickly and studied hard. Most kids would have broken, but not Austin...God, I love him.

It took me a few days to bounce back, but as I've said many times, I felt this episode was a springboard for my recovery. After I was discharged, I was determined to attend Austin's football game the following Saturday—and I did. I even managed to make my way to the bleachers without wearing the wheels off my walker. I wanted to get a part of my life back and, more importantly, reassure Austin his mother was going to be OK.

I continued outpatient rehab three days a week. And I graduated from OT first! Then several weeks later I graduated speech therapy after reading my heartfelt letter of appreciation out loud to Debbie. All three of us were in tears before I finished it, but what a moment—a moment I will never forget. For Christmas that year, I printed my letter and framed it for Debbie.

A defining moment during my recovery was transitioning from my walker to a cane. We had tried this while I was in inpatient rehab, and I was a wobbly mess on the cane. I just couldn't do it—then. A friend who owns a pharmacy had some canes in stock and sent me a black and orange one (the colors of my alma mater where I worked) with some bling and sparkle on it. I loved it! Still have it!

Soon thereafter, I was able to cut back on my 24/7 care to just during the day. Before long, I didn't need them any more. It was

AND I DID...

another significant accomplishment, although many of my friends didn't think I was ready. But what did they know? Oh, and being able to drive again? Yay! That too was a *big* moment for me, BIG, HUGE. Then days before my forty-third birthday (April 1, 2013), I was finally discharged from PT. Also during this time, I returned to work the Monday after Thanksgiving (2012)—on a cane, but I was back. There were many exciting accomplishments that were a part of my recovery, but not everything to come was an exhilarating time in my life.

CHAPTER 26

It's amazing the number of people who genuinely ask me how I've managed to endure all I have in only a few years and maintain a smile on my face, a positive attitude, and—most of all—my faith and trust in God. My answer is simple—it's God. But you know what? As simple as that sounds, it has taken many difficult times to realize He truly is the answer. Even I have asked myself why a gracious and loving God would allow me to go through some of my hardships. Surely if He loved me, He would not let all these things happen to me, right? I mean, after all, doesn't loving me mean He wants my life to be easy and comfortable? Well, no, it doesn't.

Remember, Romans 8:28? I've shared it with you twice already, for good reason. All of life's hardships are part of "all things." As a believer, I trust all of my trials and tribulations must have a divine purpose. But when I found myself in the throes of my adversities, those words were hard to believe and accept at times.

But after I accepted and realized my adversities were part of God's plan for my life, I was reminded I am to live my life to glorify God. As a result, my faith has been made sure by the trials I've experienced because *I can do all things through Christ, who strengthens me* (Philippians 4:13). Did you realize trials can develop Godly character? Well, they certainly can—plus they can enable us to *rejoice in our sufferings, because we know that suffering produces perseverance; perseverance, character; and character, hope. And hope does not disappoint us, because God has poured out his love into our hearts by the Holy Spirit, whom he has given us*" (Romans 5:3-5). Remember, God has given us His Word as a guide, His Holy Spirit to support us, and the ability to seek Him in prayer anytime and anywhere. God also promised us no trial will test us beyond our ability to bear it (1 Corinthians 10:13). I had a friend once give me a quote that read "God won't give me more than I can handle...I just wish He didn't trust me so much." I love that quote.

And finally, I believe God's purpose in our times of trouble is to teach us lessons to build us up. While we are riding the storms of life, it is important we see our times of distress as opportunities and joy through times of troubles. These are times to trust Him and learn valuable lessons as well as times to grow in maturity and strength. And maybe most importantly, these are times to better our lives so we may become the people we are capable of being for our benefit and His glory. Once we've weathered the storm, then we see the great promises fulfilled and how necessary our trials actually were.

Now, when storms of life come my way, I'm better prepared as I've learned to adjust my sails. One of my favorite quotes is by Elizabeth Edwards: "She stood in the storm, and when the wind did not blow her way, she adjusted her sails." I know difficult times will either overwhelm me, dragging me under, or define me, allowing me to become the person Christ wants me to be. And you know what? As difficult as it has been at times, I've managed to choose the latter, because I try to see hardships as opportunities to gain more strength and maturity in my Christian life and most importantly to glorify God—and I did. And I will.

CHAPTER 27

A few weeks after being discharged from inpatient therapy, my caregiver and I returned home after one of Austin's football games. As we pulled in the driveway, a constable pulled in behind us. Shortly after that, one of our neighbors pulled in. *Something's up!* Not to my surprise, Mom had been taken to the hospital, but she did not want me to know. Again, not to my surprise. That's Mom! Ironically, both my neighbor and the constable obviously knew Mom had been transported, as she asked them not to tell me. Thank goodness they both agreed they should tell me when I got home. They knew she'd forgive them...eventually. Before I could even get in the house, my cousin David was calling to tell me, as well. And Mom thought she could make it there and back without my knowledge! So, off to the hospital we went.

This was the first of several trips to the hospital for Mom. After her oncologist found more lesions in her back from the multiple myeloma, Mom agreed to more radiation treatments, as she was going as often as she could. Unfortunately, the treatments only seemed to make her pain worse. So, once her pain became more than she could handle, she would have to go to the ER. Sometimes they would treat her then send her home. Other times, they would admit her for a couple to several days in an attempt to reduce or even alleviate her pain. But unfortunately, it seemed that nothing was helping. This was the point when she became so tired and began considering to discontinue chemo…well, you know the rest of the story.

It was a long and difficult three months caring for Mom, as I too continued my outpatient physical therapy, trying to overcome my walking infirmities—and of course, Austin was my main priority. But I knew God would provide—and He did. My trust in Him was probably as strong as ever at this point in my life. After all the tough times, I had learned to depend on God, which strengthened my personal relationship with Him, allowing me to fully put my faith and trust in Him.

Think about it—I was putting my entire faith, trust, and hope in someone with whom I have a spiritual relationship and know. But how many of us trust people we barely know or don't know at all? Did you know the pilot of the plane the last time you flew? Or the chef who prepared your dinner at your favorite restaurant last night? Or the school bus driver who picks up your child in the mornings and brings him or her home in the afternoons? Although we don't always know these people, we trust them, right?

So, if we can trust all of these people, how can we not trust someone with whom we continue to build a relationship? Someone who created the heavens and the earth and all there is and who even sent His one and only son to die on the cross for us. Who sent His son for us—me and you—so we can have eternal life if—and only if—we accept Him as our Savior and repent of our sins. If you don't remember anything else in this book, remember God loves you…no matter what you've done. His grace is sufficient. He wants you to choose to live for Him so you can have life everlasting.

So, where was I? Oh yes! Finally, new chapters in my life were beginning.

CHAPTER 28

After 43 years, I bought a house in town—in town, where I longed to be. Three minutes from anywhere. I continue to thank God for my house almost every time I leave and arrive in our neighborhood. Despite commuting back and forth from our home in the country to town for so long...no, I hadn't gotten used to it. Well, I didn't. I despised it more and more with each day and each trip. It seemed all Austin and I did was run the roads to school, ball practice, church, etc. Plus I always said I was the son my father never had...now, Austin? He loved the farm. But after losing Dad, it was never the same for him either. I do have fond memories of riding the tobacco setter and driving the tractor. But one of my favorite cunning moments was while hoeing thistles in the tobacco patch, I told my dad I needed to go to the bathroom and I did...with the intent of never returning nor with the need to go to the bathroom. He probably saw right through me. But the farm was his passion—a passion he shared with and was welcomed by his one and only grandson.

For me, there were just too many memories on the farm. Wherever I looked, there was Dad. I had honored my parents by living on the farm, which allowed me to be there to help my mom when my dad passed. Although I kept the farm, I had the oppor-

AND I DID...

tunity to leave it...leaving the memories behind...and to begin a new chapter in my life.

I only looked at maybe five or six houses before I made my decision. It was a brand-new house in a fairly new subdivision in town. It was two stories and had four bedrooms and three baths. Yes, maybe it was a bit much for Austin and me, but Charlotte's husband, Ray, had not given up on me finding "Mr. Right." He encouraged me to keep that in mind while I searched for my new home. Of course, I indulged him, and we shared a lot of laughs about it. But after ten years, I just didn't know.

The day I closed on the house, I drove straight there, unlocked the front door, sat on the top step, and cried—no, I bawled. I could not believe this house was mine. I couldn't help but reflect on the many events that had taken place during the last several months, the last couple of years. I could not believe that, after all this time, I finally had a beautiful house that would be a home to Austin and me—our home in town. Oh how I wished Mom and Dad could see it!

Several of my girlfriends came over to see the house that evening. We hung out in the kitchen and sat on the floors, as there was not even one piece of furniture in the house. But I did have wine glasses I had brought from my other house, and we celebrated with Moscato. Later that evening, Scott brought Austin by so the three of us could celebrate this milestone in my life.

Oh...did I fail to mention Scott?

CHAPTER 29

Remember the guy Austin met at the funeral home while we were making Mom's funeral arrangements? And the handsome guy I thanked for helping Austin look for my thought-to-be-lost phone? Well, about a month later, he sent me a friend request on Facebook. By the way, Scott just cringes when I share that part of our story—but it's true! When I saw his picture, I recognized him and accepted his request. He later messaged me, inviting Austin and me to join him for ice cream. I thought that was so sweet! Unfortunately, between his work schedule, my work schedule, Austin's ballgames, and my furniture shopping for our new house, we just couldn't work it out.

A few weeks later, I was scheduled to work an event at the college on a Sunday afternoon. That morning my president called to tell me I did not have to work the event. Honestly, I was glad to have the day off, but Austin was bummed, as I had made arrangements for him to practice basketball with the men's assistant coach at the college while I worked. I assured Austin he could still practice with the coach, as I would take advantage of a beautiful, sunny, and warm Sunday afternoon, despite the fact it was the end of February, and walk on the trail through campus.

AND I DID...

So I took Austin into the arena and told them I'd be back in about an hour. I walked thirty minutes in one direction and then turned around, with ear buds in place and in my own world. Not long after I had turned around, making my way back to campus to get Austin, this guy came jogging by me. He turned around—and it was him. The guy from the funeral home. He stopped jogging and in a few steps I had caught up with him. He said, "I thought that was you," and the conversation took off. I even told him to not let me hold him up if he wanted to resume jogging, but he insisted he was fine walking.

He asked about Austin, and I told him he was actually on campus practicing basketball. He then asked if it was OK if he saw him, and of course I said yes. So we continued to talk, making our way back to the arena.

When we walked in, Austin was still focused and practicing, so we took a seat on the bleachers, taking it all in. After a few minutes he finished and came running over. He was really glad to see Scott again. As we were leaving, I offered to take Scott back to his car, but he was a little unsure as to where he had parked. He had only been living in Greeneville since November, and this was the first time he had been on this trail. But by the way he was describing it, I thought I knew where he had parked, so no worries. After standing at my car, talking for probably 30, maybe 45 minutes, with the door open, he conceded and agreed to let me take him to his car.

As we were driving up the street to where I thought he had parked, there sat a beautiful white Mustang convertible. It was so clean and shiny it looked like it had just rolled off the showroom floor. And guess what? It was his. As he got out, Austin was dying of thirst and invited Scott to join us at McDonald's. He hesitantly accepted, as he did not want to intrude. I assured him it was fine and told him to jump back in, and he could just ride with us. And he did.

We spent close to two hours at McDonald's with several cups of ice water, talking and getting to know each other. The date was Sunday, February 24, and I knew I would marry this man. I know...sounds crazy, right? But I knew. I learned he was a man of God and a Marine. That was all I needed to know. How I wish Mom and Dad were here to meet him.

CHAPTER 30

As I drove Scott back to his car, I asked if I could take him by our soon-to-be new home. He loved it. I wondered if he loved it enough to live there one day...I really did. Then when I took him back to his car, I gave him a copy of my book, *Only to Susan*, which I just happened to have in the car. And we said our goodbyes.

From that date forward, we saw each other almost every day. We were inseparable. And Austin? He absolutely loved Scott. He loved being with him as much as I did. It didn't take me long to realize Austin probably needed Scott as much as I did—or more.

Scott was here and more than willing to help us move into our new home. He was more than willing to do anything to help us. It was so incredible to have a man in my life. The dreams I had lived out in my heart for ten years were coming true...they were coming true, and I was falling in love. Don't tell me you don't believe in love at first sight!

CHAPTER 31

Several of my friends were worried I was falling in love too fast, but they didn't know Scott well, nor did they know my heart. Only God and I knew my heart. But that's what friends are for, right? Kind of like your parents? They may give you their opinion on something, but then the ultimate decision is up to you.

Of course, everyone who met Scott loved him. He was perfect in every way. Was he worth the wait? No doubt. Charlotte and Ray, who had become like my parents, loved Scott. Check. My "big sis" Debbie loved Scott. Check. Those were my main concerns, but Debbie told me if I married him before six months, she'd kick my you-know-what!

I don't know I ever truly believed in love at first sight. I've heard of stories like this, but now it was my story. It happened to me. It really does happen. Was I scared? Not at all. I knew—I knew he was the man for me and for Austin. And Scott reminds me and others he met and fell in love with Austin first—and he did.

My best friend, Donna, who lives in Kentucky—I miss her so much. After growing up in Greeneville, her husband accepted a job in Kentucky several years ago. We don't get to see each other enough, nor do we get to talk to each other enough. But every time we do talk or see each other, we just pick up where we left

AND I DID...

off. I finally got around to calling Donna to tell her about "this guy." It wasn't long into our conversation before I was in tears as she told me something I didn't know. Donna told me she had told her mother after I lost my mom she was going to pray diligently for God to send someone to me and Austin—and He did. I had no idea she had been praying this prayer. Needless to say, we were both in tears as we celebrated yet another answered prayer.

CHAPTER 32

Scott had knee surgery in March. Unfortunately, I had meetings that day, which were scheduled BS (before Scott) and which I was required to attend, so I could not take the day off. But I did leave home early enough to see him before surgery, and I saw him at lunch before he was discharged. Then I helped take care of him until he was up on his own.

On March 14, Austin and I gave Scott a birthday party at our home.

On April 1, Scott and Austin threw me a surprise birthday party at our home. And did I mention Scott loves to cook? Plus, I quickly realized Scott also loved to entertain—how awesome is that?

On May 11, we had the personal property estate auction at my parents'. I decided to keep the farm and our houses for the time being, mainly for Austin's sake. It was amazing the number of people who were at the auction and the amount of items to auction. The auction started at 10 am and concluded at 7:30 pm. The auctioneers never stopped, and at one point, there were two auctions taking place simultaneously. The auctioneer told me it was the biggest personal property auction they'd ever done.

AND I DID...

Several people had told me since both houses were empty now, I needed to get some renters in there. The only way to get people in the houses was to get rid of the stuff in the houses. And there was a lot of stuff. My parents kept everything—everything.

It was a day of mixed emotions. One minute I was crying, the next minute I was smiling. As I looked over the property at the hundreds of people roaming around and the cars parked on both sides of the road, I thought what a tribute to my parents this was. Then at the end of the auction, a double rainbow formed, as we'd had to contend with a few rain showers throughout the day. It was so beautiful, so radiant, and so close...I honestly thought I could touch it. Everyone who was still there was in awe and taking pictures, including me. Scott and I sat on the back of a truck bed. He was holding me in his arms as I was taking it all in. Tears were rushing down my cheeks. Everybody there came by and told me what I was thinking...it was like Mom and Dad's confirmation. It was one of the most surreal moments in my life.

Later that evening, we were at my house, having a rather deep conversation about us. All of a sudden, Scott told me to wait...he'd be right back. When he returned, he got down on one knee, with a stunning diamond ring in hand, and proposed. As tears flooded my eyes, I said, "Yes, yes!" He had intended to propose during our upcoming trip to Wilmington, NC during Memorial Day, but....

We immediately began talking about wedding plans. We both wanted a small, private ceremony, and then a huge celebration with all of our family and friends. As we began looking at dates, we realized August 24 was on a Saturday—six months to the day since we met—perfect! We'd get married in a chapel with a small, intimate ceremony downtown, and then have our celebration party afterwards at the club. And remember, my "big sis" said she'd kick my you-know-what if I got married before we had hit the six-month mark! But, oh my God—He is making my dream come true!

CHAPTER 33

At the end of May, Scott took me to Wilmington, NC, to Wrightsville Beach, where he had lived prior to moving to Greeneville. It was beautiful. Not touristy at all. There were very few people around, and it was Memorial Day.

The first morning we were there, we went for a walk on the beach, stretched before and after, did our toning exercises, and then went down to play tennis. Although it had been a couple of months since Scott's surgery, I was still concerned about his knee, but he told me it felt great. After almost every dead ball, I'd ask Scott if his knee was OK, and he assured me it was. But after several games into the set, Scott went down–hard. Oh my God–no!

I dropped my racquet and sprinted to his side. I screamed, "Your knee?" He replied, "No, I tore my Achilles!" For only a second, I was relived. Then I realized he was in excruciating pain. What should I do? And how did he know? He knew because he had torn the other one several years ago, and the feeling when he tore it was identical–like a baseball hit him in the back of the leg. Last time, he'd had to have surgery, so we were fearful that would be the case now.

AND I DID...

I called his orthopedic doctor to get his advice. He told us to go on to the ER there so he could be examined and get a boot, but there was no need for it to ruin our week if we wanted to stay, as nothing would change until we got home to see him. So I managed to get him into the Mustang. Thank God it was a beautiful day. I put the top down, which made it easier getting him in the car—Scott is a tall guy! We got to the ER, and after about an hour, we left—in a boot and on crutches.

Scott is so tough. He was determined to not let it spoil our week, and it didn't. He also guaranteed me he would not be wearing a boot when we got married. I was thinking, *Yeah, we'll see.* We didn't chance going down to the beach any more, as there was a pretty significant drop as you exited the condo property onto the beach. Consequently, we were at the poolside the rest of the week and had it pretty much all to ourselves. Then we'd go out like every night. Plus, I had the luxury of driving his Mustang and chauffeuring Scott around the rest of the week.

By the way, did I fail to mention I had him 5-1 in the first set of our tennis match? A game we have yet to finish—but we will.

While we were still enjoying our get-away vacation, Scott met the nicest gentleman. His name? Retired 86-year-old Navy Commander Paul Canada. I had noticed him earlier in the week when we were sitting poolside. As he had entered the pool area, he saluted the flag. He couldn't see well or hear well, and he was a widower. He owned one of the condos close to the one we had rented for the week. After observing him for a short time, Scott pegged him. He told him he bet he was a commander in the Navy and was listening to books as he carried a CD player in his hand while wearing headphones. And guess what? Scott was right. We both just fell in love with Commander Canada and vowed we'd stay in touch.

The next day, Scott had me drive us up to Camp Lejeune, as it was only about 40 minutes north of where we were staying. I was so excited! Camp Lejeune is not only where Scott had been stationed for most of his military career, but it was where my father was stationed, as well. We were able to enter base and drive around. It was incredibly amazing...so large! Nothing at all like I had anticipated.

After spending several hours there, knowing that was where my father and Scott had been stationed, while we were headed back, I had an epiphany. I wanted to get married on Wrightsville Beach. It was close enough to Camp Lejeune...it just all resonated with me, and Scott could not have been happier.

CHAPTER 34

With only a few months to plan our beach wedding, it was incredibly helpful Scott knew so many people there. I would tell him what I wanted, and then he would contact Army First Sergeant Ken Pike, who was a personal and close friend of his, and between the two of them, they would make it happen. He was quite the wedding planner. Even though it was a small wedding, there was so much to do!

But wait! Austin would be in school August 24. So, after we received Debbie's blessings, we decided to get married on August 10, two weeks shy of our six-month anniversary. Then we would have our wedding celebration at home at our country club on August 24. And we did.

I almost thought we were going to have to make another trip to Wilmington before the wedding, but we didn't. We just planned on spending our family vacation at the beach the week prior. This meant we'd get married on Saturday and return home on Sunday. Yes, we did it backwards. But you know me—typically the exception, not the rule!

We arrived late on Sunday evening. Having spent much of the day on Monday running errands for the wedding, I longed to be on the beach. But there were little things to be done, like obtaining our marriage license. We also met with our minister for lunch on Tuesday at the same location we were having our dinner following the wedding. He was a Navy Lieutenant Commander. As we enjoyed a delightful lunch, we discussed the wedding ceremony, using what we had at hand. I was the saltshaker. Scott was the pepper. Austin was the ketchup. The minister was a packet of Sweet 'N Low.

Our friends Jeff and Allison arrived on August 9, as did my "big sister" Debbie and her husband Mike. We played on the beach before taking everyone to dinner in downtown Wilmington along the Cape Fear River. We exchanged our wedding gifts to and from one another. And to have Jeff, Allison, Mike, Debbie, and, of course, Austin be a part of it just made it complete.

On the morning of the tenth, we had our own Bloody Mary reception on the beach as we conducted our rehearsal—in our bathing suits. It was a beautiful day and possibly the hottest day of the week. After rehearsal, Allison and Jeff hosted a picnic simultaneously on the beach and poolside—which only they could pull off—until it was time to get ready.

Scott had made arrangements for a limo to take Allison, Debbie, and me to a spa to get our hair and makeup done. We had the best "girl" time...complete with mimosas! And upon returning to the condo to get dressed, Scott had set up a buffet big enough for his entire Marine platoon, but it was just for us three girls so we wouldn't get hungry before dinner. Two things about Scott—he is incredibly thoughtful and very observant. Like, I may not realize he actually heard me say something unintentionally, but he does, and he does not forget.

CHAPTER 35

It was a beautiful, fairy tale wedding...a military wedding...on the beach...at sunset. The temperature was so nice after a very hot day.

The men got ready in Commander Canada's condo while we girls got ready in our condo. When Austin arrived in our room, he stopped me in my tracks. He looked so handsome...so grown up... in his dress blues Scott had ordered him. He even had one medal on his jacket—code of good conduct, presented by Gunny Sergeant Scotty Lynn Teague.

Before we began our escort to the entrance we had chosen at the hotel next door for the wedding party, Scott also came by our room. We sat where he and I could not see each other, and with Austin in the middle, we held hands, and Scott prayed. It was the most precious moment—I will never forget it.

At the appropriate time, Debbie, Austin, and I made our way down to the limo for our ride next door. After waiting only a few minutes, on her cue, Debbie began making her way down our selected path to the beach, followed by me on Austin's arm. Along our way, people were cheering from the poolside and from the balconies, and we weren't even married yet! As we arrived at the gazebo, it was the first time Scott and I saw each other since us girls left for the spa. I paused more than a moment, as it was the first time I'd seen Scott in his dress blues, complete with his decorated medals. Among them—a Silver Star. I stepped out of my wedding flip-flops, and then Austin proceeded to escort me down the steps onto the beach where gentlemen in uniform awaited, including our minister. But one in particular, in his dress blues, I was about to marry.

I carried a bouquet of calla lilies and two red roses. I placed the roses on two seats in the front row in memory of my parents. How I wished they could be here, especially my daddy, watching his little girl marry a Marine.

It was a lovely ceremony at sunset, officiated by Navy Lieutenant Commander Steve Hall. Austin, Scott, and I exchanged family vows. Scott and I wrote and recited our own vows to one another. Debbie, who was my matron of honor, did not drop the rings in the sand—thank God. We played "When God Made You" by Newsong over the Bose, and I just wanted to dance as I listened to every word. And for a moment, it felt like it was just the two of us. It was perfect...a fairy tale was coming true.

As we were announced as Mr. and Mrs. Scotty Teague, we made our way through the saber arch, complete with Army Captain Earl Walker, Army First Lieutenant Mike McCarthy, Navy Master Chief Malcolm Swain, Marine Corps Master Sergeant Donald Cummings, Army Staff Sergeant Gene Funderburk, and Army Sergeant Ken Fowler. But as we approached the last two gentleman, they lowered their sabers. Confused, I looked at Scott, wondering what was going on. First Sargent Ken Pike, who oversaw the saber sword detail, ordered Gunny Teague to kiss his wife. And he did. Then First Sergeant Pike ordered again, but in a deeper, louder, more commanding voice, "Gunny Teague! I said kiss your bride!" Scott took me in his arms, dipped me, and kissed me like never before. The last two sabers were raised, then I surprisingly got smacked on the butt with a saber by USMC

AND I DID...

Master Sergeant Cummings, as the gentleman said, "Welcome to the Marine Corps, Mrs. Teague!" It was awesome!

Hundreds of strangers gathered on the beach to watch this decorated wedding taking place, but among our personal guests were a blanket of many military personnel, both active duty and veterans. Afterwards, we hosted a dinner for all of our invited guests to celebrate this momentous occasion, and among our guests was Commander Canada. Remember him? He even rode in the limo with us to dinner. Following our celebration dinner, the limo took Jeff, Allison, Austin, Scott, and me downtown as we strolled the streets of downtown Wilmington before calling it a night.

CHAPTER 36

I prayed for ten years for God to give me a husband with whom I was equally yoked. And He did. I told myself I was setting my bar high for the man of my dreams. And I did. Speaking of praying and waiting and putting my full faith and trust in God...I told myself I would be able to deal with the loss of my father. And I did. I told myself I would fight back and overcome my infirmities from my stroke—rather, my "event." And I did. I told myself I would be able to accept the loss of my mother. And I did. I told myself I would overcome my battle with depression. And I did. I told myself I would be able to take care of the farm and our houses. And I did. Amazing what you can do when you submit yourself to God's timing and God's plan!

As we packed up the next morning, as Mr. and Mrs. Teague—and Austin, of course—with our shining rings on our left hands and sun-kissed tans, we began our journey home as a family. But it wasn't long before we were all reminded of the battle awaiting us at home. I'm sorry, did I not mention? I was diagnosed with breast cancer just days before we left for our wedding.

About the Author

Susan D. Crum — keynote speaker, author, coach, and consultant, continues to lead and support entrepreneurs in creating their own online businesses, as well as developing positive leadership among teams, businesses, and organizations with her experience and expertise around the world. In addition, she has a heart and passion to inspire and encourage women as they toil in their lives to prepare for and overcome adversity. For Susan, this ministry has been received, not achieved. Where she is, is where God has placed her. Susan graduated from South Greene High School in 1988 and Tusculum College in 1991 with a degree in business administration. In 2005, she received her certification in Non-Profit Management from the University of Tennessee and enjoyed eighteen successful years in the non-profit sector before becoming an entrepreneur.

Susan is a native of Greene County and is a 10-year breast cancer survivor. Previously, she founded her own 501c3 foundation and women's ministry, Tapestry of Faith. She is engaged to Pete Thacker and has one son, Austin, a bonus-daughter, Hannah, and is a grammie to Scarlett. Susan and Pete attend Christ Fellowship and together they enjoy traveling, going to the beach, playing golf, attending Atlanta Braves games, Tennessee athletic events, fishing, live music and collecting quotes. She often refers to herself as a quote-a-holic! Plus, she's been known to get a little over zealous about the colors pink and orange!

Email: susandcrum@gmail.com
Connect with Susan D. Crum on
Facebook, Instagram, LinkedIn, or Twitter.

www.ingramcontent.com/pod-product-compliance
Lightning Source LLC
Chambersburg PA
CBHW032019040426
42448CB00006B/660